"Well…It Looks…Bettr'n It Did"

"Well...It Looks...Bettr'n It Did"

◆

A Modern American Odyssey

D. Wassom

iUniverse, Inc.
New York Lincoln Shanghai

"Well…It Looks…Bettr'n It Did"
A Modern American Odyssey

Copyright © 2005 by David Clarke Wassom

All rights reserved. No part of this book may be used or reproduced by any means, graphic, electronic, or mechanical, including photocopying, recording, taping or by any information storage retrieval system without the written permission of the publisher except in the case of brief quotations embodied in critical articles and reviews.

iUniverse books may be ordered through booksellers or by contacting:

iUniverse
2021 Pine Lake Road, Suite 100
Lincoln, NE 68512
www.iuniverse.com
1-800-Authors (1-800-288-4677)

ISBN-13: 978-0-595-35477-1 (pbk)
ISBN-13: 978-0-595-79969-5 (ebk)
ISBN-10: 0-595-35477-7 (pbk)
ISBN-10: 0-595-79969-8 (ebk)

Printed in the United States of America

Contents

JUST A NOTE.. vii
DEAR READER...................................... xi
HOW CAN YOU TELL A HAPPY MOTORCYCLE RIDER?...... 1
MOON OVER MENTONE............................. 3
THE JOURNEY BEGINS............................. 4
THE JOURNEY CONTINUES......................... 6
OH, THANK HEAVEN FOR DR. PEPPER............... 8
THE REST STOP................................... 9
AND NOW THE REST OF THE JOURNEY.............. 11
WE ARRIVE TO SOME SURPRISES!................. 14
GREEN EGGS AND HAM........................... 15
THE ADVENTURE BEGINS......................... 17
WHY?... 21
WE CLEAN HOUSE............................... 23
WE RE-OPEN THE RESTAURANT................... 27
"I DID, TOO!"-"WHAT?"......................... 29
"GREASE"...................................... 31
HOTEL SNIPPETS................................ 33
WAITRESSES 35

WORKING HARD?.	39
WE PICK OUR ROOM.	41
WE LEARN OUR LESSON-THE 3 R'S	43
FLORA AND FAUNA	45
WHO ROOTS FOR WHOM?—OR MYOPIA	47
"ISMS"	48
WELL-IT LOOKS BETTER'N IT DID!	51
THE OLD OAK TREE	54
MENTONE	57
MOVING ON THE CHEAP!	59
THE BIG FLICK	60
HONESTY HAS ITS OWN REWARDS.	63
SOUTHERN ANNOYANCES	65
THE HONEYMOANERS	69
SCOUNDRELS	70
OUT OF TOUCH-OR THE GENERATION GAP	73
HYPOCRISY	75
HOW CAN DRYNESS BE SO WET?	77
RACE	80
"GOOD OL' BOY SYNDROME"	83
THE ROOF	85
GREAT EXPECTATIONS	88
ALL GOOD THINGS MUST END	90
"LET ME MOW ON IT"	94

JUST A NOTE

We took the Cover Photo as a "gag" for our Western friends, who thought "We'd died and gone to Hell" when we moved to Alabama. Stereotypes abound everywhere you go, so we thought we'd "ham it up a bit for them" with a Southern stereotype. (The beard is real. I shaved it off right after the photo was taken).

We sent the photo to friends as a Christmas Card in 2001, and it did get quite a few laughs. The back cover shows us as we really look.

ACKNOWLEDGMENT

The Cable Company just expanded our service from 24 to 79 channels. In spite of the myriad of new offerings, I still haven't been able to find anything that captivates my attention. My housecat, "Schitzie", just jumped up into my lap; and that captured my attention for the moment. It's fall and the sun is going down earlier every night, and there is less outdoors to do. I refuse to become a computer addict, so out of desperation for something to do, I decided to claim my "moment of fame" and become a "famous author".

They often say, "Fact is stranger than fiction;" and having been privy to some interesting experiences, I have decided to share them with you.

I wish to give special thanks to my dear wife, Claudia, who has put up with me through all of this. Special thanks to Charlotte Rice who edited and typed this up so it would be legible. I would be remiss not to acknowledge my chair side Dental Assistant of over 20 years-Cindy Burkhalter, who on several occasions told me that I had a knack for writing and that I ought to write something.

Well, Cindy-"Better late than never".

DEAR READER

This is really the Foreword to my book. I'm, however, making it my First Chapter because my wife contends that, "No one ever reads Forewords."

Change Happens!! I started this book with the intention, the idea, and the thought, that a Foreword wasn't necessary. This book is my story. Everything I write about really did happen. It is a compilation of vignettes along with observation and commentary.

My dear wife Claudia, who has the best intentions, often likes to play the "Devil's Advocate". She would say, "Well, I don't think you ought to write about this," or; "I don't think you ought to write about that, because you might offend someone." Or she would say, "I don't think you ought to mention people's names, because those involved may not like it."

I love Claudia dearly, but in my attempt to heed her advice, and after getting half the way through my book, I became very frustrated. True, there are a few things that belong to my story that may offend a few people; but if I leave them out, then the story doesn't get told!

"Tabloids get sued all the time for writing about people, and we don't need to get sued," she said.

"Well, this is not a tabloid. Tabloids look for sensationalism, and will tell half truths, use innuendoes, twist the truth, or outright make something up in order to get readers' attention," I said.

"But the truth sometimes hurts," she said.

"I know," I replied, "but consider the contrary-when someone has done something to be proud of-the truth uplifts, empowers and can make one free. Should we, out of fear of offending a few, suppress what we know to be true?"

Therefore, I offer this disclaimer. I write in an attempt to laugh with, and not at, anyone! I write the truth, what really happened-nothing is made up. I do comment on things from my personal perspective, since it would be hard to write from someone else's personal perspective. Should anyone take offense about what I write-please, that is their prerogative. Please forgive! I only have good intentions.

In this writing, I have omitted names in order to avoid potential conflict. In many cases, I use real names. Now-"Damn the Torpedoes-Full Speed Ahead!"

We decided that it was time for a change; and since that decision was made, our lives have been anything but mundane. It was a change for the good.

HOW CAN YOU TELL A HAPPY MOTORCYCLE RIDER?

How can you tell a happy motorcycle rider? We've all heard this one haven't we? "By the bugs on his teeth, of course." Well, we've got a better one!

It was a lazy, warm, summer afternoon-midweek-slow time. We were basically alone in the Hotel, when we heard a noise out in the parking lot. It got louder. Sure enough-anyone who knows bikes is familiar with the telltale deep-throated sound of a Harley. I don't know bikes, and I'm familiar with the deep-throated sound of a Harley. So we were motivated to move to the door to take a peek. It was a beautiful bike! Chopped-Long fork, but not too long-Purple with gold trim-Lots of chrome! But it wasn't the bike that caught our immediate attention. No sirree! The driver wore his leathers over a dark suit. But what sat on the back of the bike was astonishing. Tall, Blond, Beautiful-wearing a full wedding gown, complete with veil. It was a sight to behold! Unusual to say the least.

With jaws dropped in astonishment, we asked if we could be of assistance? They had just gotten married in Chattanooga, were on their honeymoon, and did we have a room? Of course we had a room! (We were running on empty as far as guests were concerned.) As they approached us, Claudia noticed something quite peculiar. There were bugs in the bride's toile! (Pronounced tool-your know, that lacy stuff that you make bride's gowns and veils out of). Lots Of Bugs! Claudia must have spent the next 15 or 20 minutes helping to remove the bugs. Our motorcycle rider had to be ver-r-r-r-y happy! No! Not because of the bugs on his teeth, nor not really because of the bugs in his bride's toile. She was, in my estimation, quite the dish and worthy of anybody's catch. And the two of them appeared to be quite obviously in love. After the cleaning task was accomplished, and after having inquired about where to procure a nice meal, the couple, still clad in their finery, mounted the Harley and drove off-veil fluttering in the wind. Upon their return, more bug removal took place!

MOON OVER MENTONE

We had the privilege, on several occasions, of hosting a young couple from California. She had a part in a TV Soap Opera and he was a stockbroker. Her parents live in Fort Payne; and when she came to visit them, they would stay at the Mentone Springs Hotel.

It was a lazy midweek morning. We were not particularly busy, nor was the Town of Mentone-Very quiet-Not much going on-But not for long!

It seems that our young soap star had gone out to the parking lot to get something from their car. The room that the young couple had booked was directly above, and looked out onto the parking lot. It also seems that our young stockbroker was plotting some personal mischief. He was still in the room that overlooked the parking lot, and therefore their car. He was in the process of attracting his girlfriend's attention by having dropped his pants, and having hung his bare derriere out the window. He thought he was giving his friend a "private showing". Little did he know that just then, Judy was coming out the door of the White Elephant Galleries. She saw the "Full Moon" in all its shining glory. And Claudia was also going out of the Hotel to go see Judy. She was disappointed that, from her perspective, she only saw half a moon. I understand that after this all occurred, that it just wasn't his moon that was shining. He had a glowing red face.

THE JOURNEY BEGINS

◆

March 17, 1996

"Let me tell you a story 'bout a man named Jed", Randy sang as we pulled out of 350 McDuff Avenue. My stepson's words were so appropriate. My pickup had been piled high with various personal belongings that would have toppled out had it not been for the myriad of ropes and bungee cords that were denying gravity its due course. It would not have been hard to mistake it for the one Jed Clampett drove to Hollywood. I even had my faithful dog, Haggie (pronounced Hoggy), with me on the front seat-big dog, mixed breed, over 100 pounds, very sweet personality.

In the Jeep Cherokee was Claudia. The Cherokee, including the floor and seat spaces, was stuffed full of more of our personal paraphernalia. We did leave the front passenger seat available for Odie-Claudia's mixed breed, 50 pound, 14-year old "poodlesque poochie".

The original plan called for us to tow one vehicle behind the other, and we would spell each other off at driving. Try as we might, we could fit no more into the moving truck! Do we leave "stuff" behind? That's all it was-just "stuff". It could be replaced-or could it? It seems sometimes things that have very little intrinsic value do manage to attach themselves to us, and that appeared to be the case with our "stuff". It stuck to us more than we were willing to admit. So-a last minute decision-a trip to Radio Shack to procure walkie-talkies. No spelling each other off, but at least we could communicate with each other. And most important of all-we had our "stuff"!

It was an uneventful seven-hour drive to Temecula. We accomplished all the required food stops, gas stops, potty stops, and dog stops. We visited a while with my sister, Kathy; and we retired early, because we were planning on a good, long drive tomorrow. Little did we know!

THE JOURNEY CONTINUES

Up early, quick breakfast, a brief visit with Betty Camp in Hemet and then on to Highway 10. (By the way, Betty is quite the gal. At this writing, she is 89, still drives and is quite the social butterfly). We knew our final destination, but we had no set itinerary-except for stopping at Claudia's daughter's home in Houston.

As our convoy made its way east, the walkie-talkies proved to be a godsend.

"Please slow down, dear. My pickup can't keep up with you on this steep hill."

"Do you need a potty break? I do."

"I'm hungry, are you? Let's stop and eat."

"I think Haggie needs to go. She didn't go at the last stop."

"I'm getting tired. I think I need some caffeine."

"I need a potty break!"

"Did you see that rude truck driver cut me off?"

"Let's eat."

"I found a good "oldies" station. Tune to 1040am."

"Okay."

"Odie needs a potty break."

"Are you getting tired, dear?"

"Shall we find some place to stop for the night?"

"No, I'm okay. Let's keep going."

Before we knew it, it was getting late; and we found ourselves in El Paso, Texas where we all took a potty break. So far, we had made good time, had taken all the necessary stops-even a chance now and then to stretch our legs and stretch the dogs' legs. But we were getting tired!

Claudia insisted, however, that we "NOT STAY THE NIGHT IN EL PASO"! She and her late husband had had a bad experience there years earlier, when a would-be car thief apparently could not hotwire their diesel pickup but left evidence of his activities. And, needless to say, my pickup was an open invitation to a "please help yourself" party. She had visions of the contents of the truck ending up at local pawnshops, and who knows where the truck might end up. Or, how about the Jeep? It was loaded with even more valuables. I had to agree. We spotted a town that appeared to be about an hour's drive-further east. We would stop there.

The accommodations we found could hardly be considered opulent. Now, I have stayed in some places, when desperate, that I considered "dives"; but what we found had to be the worst I have ever seen. Claudia agreed. Suddenly, we "found new energy" and weren't quite as tired as we previously had thought. We agreed to drive on. On and on and on and on-an occasional gas station-an occasional ranch-nothing! The highway was becoming deserted. Even the Big Rigs seemed to have disappeared. It was now March 18 and then some. I recollect-close to 2 a.m.. We had been on the road for 18 hours.

OH, THANK HEAVEN FOR DR. PEPPER

I never have liked coffee! I don't particularly like coke! However, Dr. Pepper has long been one of my favorites. Fortunately, we had the foresight to stock up on several 6-packs of the stuff. It came in very handy.

"How are you doing, dear?"
"I'm okay. How about you?"
"I'm okay. What should we do?"
"Keep driving, I guess."
"Thank goodness for caffeine."
"Yeah."

I had lost count of just how many good old Dr. Peppers I had consumed, but I was beginning to feel like Forest Gump when he was being entertained by the President of the United States and had drunk "a whole mess of Dr. Peppers".

"What's the matter, son? Nervous?" The President asked.
"No! I gotta pee!"

I was contemplating my options at relieving myself when, out of the blue, a sign appeared! The "goddess of the late night highway" suddenly smiled on us-"REST STOP 1 MILE".

"Did you see that sign? We're stopping!"

(By the way, if you haven't-<u>Forrest Gump</u> is a must see).

THE REST STOP

As we pulled into the rest stop, I looked for signs that pointed to "VEHICLES THIS WAY>"-"<TRUCKS THIS WAY". There were none! So, I sought out a spot between two trucks with space enough for two cars to park. Claudia said she would wait while I went first-due to the urgent nature of my going. As bad as I needed to go, I had the urge to grab Haggie and her leash; and we hurried off together to the "Men's". When we stepped out, it hit me that it had become very cold. It was nearly freezing. As I approached the "Men's", I saw two seedy looking characters loitering around the entrance. I hesitated briefly, then forged ahead, feeling quite uneasy. The two were quite creepy.

One of them looked at me and said, "Wow, that's a big dog! Does he bite?"

You know, there have been numerous instances in my life when I have been asked a question, in an uncomfortable situation, which I wish I could have come out with a miraculous retort. I usually only manage to babble out something stupid or totally incoherent. Only later do I think of something remarkable-the perfect answer-and then I mentally kick myself and ask, "Now, why didn't I think of that when I needed it?"

"That's a big dog! Does he bite?"

"Only when I tell her to," I retorted.

Wow! How did I think of that? The two were taken aback a bit by my remark. I could tell that I had scored big.

We took care of business. A few minutes later we accompanied Claudia and Odie to the "Women's".

Now, there is no telling if the two strangers were up to something or not. But the thought occurred to me that, if they had been, I was lucky to have the companionship of a good friend named Haggie-just as long as the next stranger didn't know that she was a "pussy cat" and would have likely licked him to death as anything else. A dog can really be a "man's best friend".

It was now time to apply the rest stop to its intended purpose-to rest! The rest stop was full of 18-wheelers. I don't think I saw another car. I have stopped many times at rest stops in many states; but I do not recall ever having stopped, previous to or since this experience, in a rest stop with no separate parking for autos and trucks. It was time to get some needed rest and here we were sandwiched in between 18-wheelers! The trucks' engines were all idling away-with their drivers tucked away in the sound proof cabs and sleeping berths. They were obviously sleeping.

"Klackety, klacety, klackety, klackety," went the idling diesel engines. Sleepity, sleepity, sleepity, could we not! The noise wasn't deafening, but it was too loud and annoying to relax. We were trapped in a lair of snorting dragons. We were unanimous in this. It was time to make an escape. Drive on, we did. Drink more Dr. Pepper, we did.

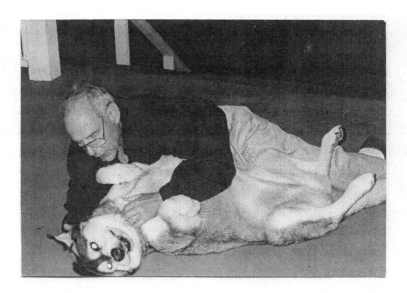

"Haggie" plays with hotel guest

AND NOW THE REST OF THE JOURNEY

Thank heavens for the walkie-talkies! I really don't think we could have kept going without them. Just being able to talk-talk about anything-helped allay the boredom and sleeplessness. We drove on and on some more, stopped at an all night gas station, and walked the dogs and ourselves. As we continued, the blackness started to show hues of purple-then orange-then red-then "Ouch"! The hot morning sun was burning directly into my eyes. We were heading due east into the sun. Not a cloud in the sky! I had to shade my eyes with one hand and hoped that the other was really steering us down the middle of the road. Maybe it was due to my stressed out condition-maybe not, but I have never encountered a morning sun that was harder to drive with in my life! Claudia had the same experience. We kept going. Stopping for breakfast, gas, dogs, and the other.

San Antonio! San Antonio? We were in San Antonio! I wasn't interested in stopping to see the Alamo or the River Walk. We had made it to San Antonio, and the faster we put it behind us the better. (I've never been in San Antonio before, or since; but if I ever make it back, I'll stop and see the attractions).

We were only a few hours from Houston! We could almost smell it. We suddenly had renewed energy. My sense of well being did not last long; and as we arrived in Houston, I was in some sort of a daze. I'm not really sure how it feels to be a Zombie, but I'm sure I felt like one.

"We didn't expect you until tomorrow," exclaimed Ginger.

"Neither did we," we tiredly replied.

It had been approximately 30 hours ago that we left Temecula. Dogs sequestered in the back yard-a short chat with Ginger-and we crashed! We slept at least 10 hours.

I drove for 16 hours once. It was from the North rim of the Grand Canyon to the San Francisco Bay area. I thought that had been my limit! Never in my wildest dreams did I ever think we would attempt a thirty-hour trip. As we stepped out of our vehicles at the end of this trip, I was really exhausted-both mentally and physically. There had been a few things I saw during the last hours of this drive that I'm not sure were really there. I know I had become a danger to myself as well as other drivers. I'll never do something so stupid again! Don't You Do It Either!

We were at it early again-about sunrise. We felt about 1,000% better after the long rest. The next leg of our journey would be easy-and mostly in daylight.

"Westward, Ho! Go West young man! The Wild, Wild West!"

The thought had just occurred to me that I couldn't think of a single bit of wisdom about going east! Yet, here we were-going directly into the morning sun-AGAIN! However, this time, it was cloudy. No sweat! Then, the thought occurred to me that the new day begins in the East. The day ends with the sun in the West. We were on a journey to start something new; so, I guess east was a good direction to go after all.

We were still on Highway 10. On to Beaumont, Texas-then Lake Charles, Louisiana-Lafayette, Louisiana-the Achafalaya Swamp Causeway-Baton Rouge. Just East of Baton Rouge, Highway 10 goes South into New Orleans. We finally left our well-driven friend to avoid going through New Orleans. Highway 12 was now our companion-only for a short while. At Slidell, we headed in a new direction-Northeast-on Highway 59. We traveled through the Southeast corner of Mississippi through such places as Piciuny, Hattiesburg, Meridian, and on to Alabama. Tuscaloosa-home of the famous Crimson Tide and the late Bear Bryant! By the time we got to Birmingham, it was still light-barely. This would be our last gas and rest stop. Yes, we were almost there! A two-hour drive to Fort Payne, Alabama. We arrived about 8 p.m. at Claudia's brother's house. A good night's sleep, and tomorrow morning we would drive the 10 miles to our final destination-Mentone, Alabama. We had bought the oldest hotel in Alabama-The Mentone Springs Hotel!

WE ARRIVE TO SOME SURPRISES!

The next morning, we leisurely got up, (no more rush), had breakfast and then on to the M.S.H. When we got there, we were surprised to find the seller's son and family still residing in the building. It turns out, to our surprise, that they do things a little different than on the West Coast. We expected to take immediate occupancy. Wrong! We had not read the fine print! The seller has 30 days after close of escrow, in Alabama, to vacate the premises.

    The occupants graciously sped up endeavors to vacate while we spent the next three nights at Gary's house. When our truck arrived, we were moving our "stuff" in while they were moving their "stuff" out. "Stuff" has its way of monopolizing one's life, doesn't it? Fortunately, we were not occupying the same spaces. Michael was living in the basement apartment, that he had previously assured us was "a wonderful place and we certainly would love living there". Only in Michael's dreams! We had previously ruled it out. It was dark, almost windowless, damp, and had short ceilings, no higher than 6' 6". For starters, I'm 6' 3"! This is the space that Norville Hall had lived in during his tenure at the hotel. I guess being short has its definite advantages. It may have been all right for Michael and Norville, but we thought it something akin to living in a cave.

GREEN EGGS AND HAM

It was a learning experience. Never having run a B&B or a restaurant, we definitely were amateurs. Early on, we decided it would be a nice touch to offer individuals a "To Order" breakfast. This has worked out really nice and is something that sets us apart from many B&Bs who do not offer a choice. We started out offering some fancy items such as crepes, but we soon found out that there was little call for such niceties. We ended up offering a good old hearty country breakfast with the following options-pancakes, waffles, French toast, blueberry pancakes, hash browns, eggs any way you like them (including any kind of omelet), bacon, ham, sausage, toast, and juices-that's about it! This breakfast menu offering has worked quite well for us. But we have refused to do grits! I'm sorry! Southerners seem to like them, but I have never ever, ever, seen a Southerner eat grits plain. They always mix them with their eggs or something else. I'm of the conviction that if an item won't stand the taste test on its own, then it isn't worth cooking, and I'm unanimous about that! So we have occasional disappointments for lack of grits.

There were occasions, when we were extremely busy, that we attempted to offer a buffet breakfast. We would set up a nice row of chafing dishes that included almost everything mentioned previously, and then some. We then proceeded in an attempt to keep them adequately stocked. Occasionally we had to do double time to keep up, for example, when one male guest took about 30 pieces of bacon for himself. I'm not kidding! What happened to his manners, and his respect for the other guests?

Early on, we also learned an interesting lesson. It appears to be a fact that, if one leaves scrambled eggs in a stainless steel chafing pan for any length of time, they begin to turn green! Quite green with time. Needless to say-not too appetizing! We learned from our mistake quickly. And from thence forth, we would put them in a Pyrex casserole dish, and then place the casserole inside the chafing pan. As such, the eggs did just fine.

We have thought, that had we not changed the procedure, we might have gotten a visit from "Sam I Am" to have some of our delicious "Green Eggs and Ham".

THE ADVENTURE BEGINS

Before I tell you what in the world got into us to purchase the Mentone Springs Hotel (hereafter designated by the letters M.S.H) in the first place, why we ought to have had our heads examined, and so forth, I will offer a brief history of the M.S.H. This is so you will know a little about the "what?" before the "why?"

Dr. J. Frank Caldwell of Pennsylvania built the M.S.H in 1884. It is by many accounts the "oldest Hotel in Alabama"; and it is factually one of a few remaining structures of its type-being built of solid wood. Walls, floors, ceilings, everything is made of wood. In my estimation, if a fire got going, it would probably consume the whole building in about ten minutes. Many old buildings have met their demise in just such a fashion.

Dr. Caldwell had been traveling through the area and became ill. He attributed his recovery to some spring water that he consumed. (It seems that it was quite the rage back then to find magical cures for about anything). After returning to Pennsylvania, he sold all of his belongings and moved to Mentone so he could build the Mentone Springs Hotel, and share his newly discovered cure with the populace.

The "healing powers" of the springs were apparently quite good because, by the turn of the century, it was by many accounts quite a busy place. Back then, it operated in the summer only. Winters in Mentone can be quite harsh.

Mentone also became popular with many wealthy individuals from such places as Birmingham. Many summer homes were built here so they could escape the heat. Mentone is in the southern end of the Appalachians, on top of what is known as Lookout Mountain-cooler, breezier, and less humid than the surrounding area.

The Hotel was doing so good that, in 1916, an annex with an additional 30 rooms was built-bringing the total to 80 rooms. The Hotel grounds encompassed 200 acres-complete with stables, vegetable gardens, dairy, tennis courts, homes for the employees, walking gardens and the like. Food preparation was done, as was the custom at the time, in a kitchen separate from the main building. Drinking water, of course, was brought up from the springs.

The '20s apparently roared at the M.S.H., too! Rumor has it that Al Capone would meet his Cuban contacts here. Also rumored-he "shot up" one of the rooms. Claudia thinks she found the bullet holes.

As did many concerns, the M.S.H. met her demise during the depression of the '30s. Stories go, that she was lost and won in a few card games. She was purchased by the Baptist Church and used for a time as a retreat. An individual, by the Name of Norville Hall, leased the building for a while and then purchased it in 1946. And Norville was an individual! A recluse, he lived at the M.S.H. alone for 30 years. He was an accomplished organist-traveled and performed his talents in many locations. He also repaired organs, filling the hotel with organs and organ parts. He had a large, working pipe organ of his own on the main floor. In order to accommodate the pipes, it became necessary for him to cut holes in the floors and ceilings above. Can you imagine how it must have been on a wind chilled, foggy, late night to hear organ music coming from the old, run down Hotel? It brings back memories of "Phantom Of the Opera" to my mind. Of course, neighbors were quite chagrined from time to time at the goings on. (I have this on good authority).

As far as we can tell, Norville did nothing to maintain the Hotel-only to contribute to her ruination and demise.

We have been told that, about 1979, somewhere in Minnesota, while performing at the organ, Norville Hall dropped dead. Well, we can at least assume that he died doing what he loved to do. I don't think there are many of us who will be able to claim that distinction. After his death, his organ was dismantled and sold to a church in Nashville.

Norville apparently had no legal heirs, so the Hotel sat vacant for a time. Jack Jones, one of Mentone's prominent residents, told me that he had "considered buying the Hotel and using it for firewood". Luckily, Ray and Sandra Padget came along and bought the Hotel. He was a Coca-Cola executive from Atlanta. The Padgets were responsible for a great deal of repair to the ailing Hotel They are also responsible for getting the Hotel placed on the National Register of Historic Places.

Then along came Charlie Johnson! We do not know the details of the arrangement, but this local entrepreneur struck a deal with the Padgets to restore the restaurant in the Hotel. Which He did! He hired an accomplished Chef, and we have been told that the restaurant flourished for a while. Charlie managed to pull some legal strings, and through "loop holes" in his contract with the Padgets, he became sole owner of the M.S.H. (We had the privilege of visiting with Sandra Padget one day when she stopped by the Hotel. She was not very happy with what had transpired those few years earlier). Then Charlie died! Brain tumor-I'm told. The Hotel was left, along with a number of other business enterprises, to Charlie's common law wife. Bobby, apparently overwhelmed with all the businesses she inherited, had become frustrated with the Hotel. It was not officially for sale, but the real estate agent, being aware, told us, "It might be for sale. Let me check and call you back." It was! We bought it! Spring of 1996.

Many people say, "There is no adventure in America any more." We didn't discover any gold, or combat any grizzly bears; but we found plenty of our own adventure of a different nature. We write in hopes we can share a glimpse of it with you.

Mentone Springs Hotel
(as we bought her)

WHY?

Why did we buy the M.S.H.? What would make a seemingly successful Dentist leave his practice to pursue an old Hotel? Why would a successful business lady leave her Silicone Valley job to do the same? I could go on about "how I lost everything in a nasty California divorce" and would soon be forced to file for personal bankruptcy. (The attorneys, as usual, made out very well). Or, how I had a very bad L5 disc in my back which was occupationally aggravated. Or, how I had been advised by several credible parties "to get as far from that woman (referring to my ex) as I can". I could also go on about how Claudia felt it was time for a change; and she was too close to her kids. But these are all topics for another book.

The plain fact of the matter was that, "WE WERE NUTS!"

But we did manage to rationalize that it was time for, and that we "needed a change". And, after all, neither one of us was afraid of hard work.

The sale of Claudia's home in Fremont, California enabled us to purchase a 20,000-sq. ft.-100+ year old hotel in Mentone, Alabama.

Hotel grounds..."after"

WE CLEAN HOUSE

The main floor, as previously mentioned, was in pretty good shape. We have the Pagets and Charlie to thank for that. The seven rooms in the left wing had been restored, as well as the "community baths". We were not terribly impressed with any of them except the one that we previously mentioned as having stayed in a few nights. The other rooms were screaming for some paint, floor coverings, some curtains, dressers and the like. We got to work right away on them; and after a couple of weeks, we thought that they looked marginally presentable.

We asked $39 to $59 a night, depending on the room. We had our first guests the second week we were there. The previous owner failed to tell us of the booking. In spite of the surprise, it worked out quite well.

The upstairs looked like a bomb had gone off up there! We could see some potential through it all. So we got a BIG Dumpster and started cleaning house. One room had been stacked floor to ceiling with lumber. As it turned out, all of it was from the Hotel itself. We tossed it all out of a window into the parking lot, sorted through it and kept what was usable. This is where I found bead-board to make repairs to bare walls such as the one the squirrel had used. Some wood, being of no use, made a nice evening bonfire.

One room was totally full of beer cans. Other rooms contained bales of straw, magazines, papers, doors off their hinges, old clothes, old filing cabinets, and Christmas decorations-basically a hodge-podge of peoples' junk. We even did find and threw out a useless kitchen sink. One small treasure did present itself! We found a box of old Hotel literature, including brochures and menus-really old ones from the early 1900's! Also, some pictures of Norville Hall. These items remain today with the Hotel.

I will not go into the details but, within a year, we had turned 6 rooms upstairs into 3 very nice, large guestrooms complete with private baths, gas fireplaces, and king-sized beds. We took two adjoining rooms and made a bath out of the smaller of the two, complete with old claw-foot tubs. We did all the work—hole patching, door replacing, painting—even the electrical and plumbing. We did not feel at all bad about the $69 & $79/nite charge.

Lumber we threw out the Window

WE CLEAN HOUSE

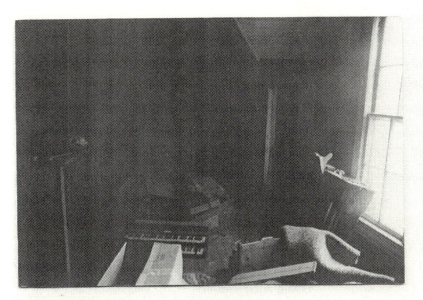

Up Stairs room Before ↑

after ↓

Dave paints the Hotel

WE RE-OPEN THE RESTAURANT

Prior to our purchase of the Hotel, a friend of my sister-in-law came to her one day and stated, "I went up to the old Hotel in Mentone for lunch, and I'm never going back."

Of course the question was, "Why not?"

The reply, "Well, that man came out of the kitchen, bare footed, bare chest, cigarette in mouth, beer can in one hand, and my meal in the other."

This story is allegedly true. I'm going to let it stand on its own with no further comment! (Except, it may give us a clue as to where the room full of empty beer cans came from).

Now you have a vague idea what we had to deal with as far as reputation goes. To get on track, we called the County Health Department. An Ansel System had to be installed in the hood for fire protection. (Side note: There was not one fire extinguisher to be found in the whole building-or smoke alarm. These were acquired).

When we quizzed the previous occupant about the lack of such devices and what they planned to do had a fire broken out, he said, "Well, we ain't had one yet."

We cleaned and painted the kitchen and rearranged some of the appliances and shelves. We hired a local, young man who had a reputation of being a good cook. We made up a menu, hired help, and called Cisco Systems with an order. Our grand opening introductory offer was a buffet for $5 a head. It was a huge success! In fact, we were so busy we couldn't keep up. Members of Claudia's family, who came to the buffet to eat, ended up helping. We stayed busy every Sunday thereafter. We had limited weekday lunch, and weekend dinner business; but all in all, for a couple of amateurs, we considered it a success!

"I DID, TOO!"- "WHAT?"

As we settled into a daily routine at the M.S.H., it was anything but routine. We entertained B&B guests when they came (mostly on weekends), ran the restaurant (mostly on weekends); and from time to time, we got quite tied up (mostly on weekends). The rest of the time we kept very busy fixing up the Old Lady. I personally painted every inch of her fading exterior, and a whole lot of her 20,000sq.ft. interior-along with repairs and aforementioned renovations.

One Friday night, as dinnertime approached, we started getting a nervous feeling. Our cook wasn't on time-then he was late-then he wasn't there. 1 was pressed into immediate service. Thank heavens we were not very busy that night; and thank heavens I had been helping out in the kitchen all along, especially on busy nights. Fortunately, 1 had a sense of the routine! I spent the next 6 years in the kitchen as "Chef Extraordinaire"!

Several days later we finally caught up with him and asked, "What happened?"

"I quit," said he.

"Well," said we, "Why didn't you give us some notice?"

"I did," said he, "I didn't show up,"

"What?" said we.

"That's how we give notice around here. We just don't show up!" said he.

"What ever happened to common courtesy and respect?" 1 asked.

He just shrugged his shoulders.

I guess we had become spoiled out West where it was a matter of routine to show a little more class. We weren't sure at the moment if he was just "pulling our chain" about this or not; but as time went on at the

M.S.H., we were "Given Notice" by several employees in the exact same manner.

By the way, I sort of liked the job 1 inherited. We got a lot of repeat customers who liked my fried chicken, my cream of mushroom soup, and my shrimp scampi.

The Kitchen and the Cook

"GREASE"

No! You will not read about John Travolta and Olivia Newton-John in this snippet!

Shortly after our arrival in Mentone, we were blessed with a visit from Claudia's brother and his friend. The four of us decided to go down to the local restaurant for dinner. So we did! The menu offered a variety of choices-beef, chicken, pork, fish. Each one of us ordered something different from this menu. When our meal arrived, it all looked the same! All breaded and deep-fried-although the menu made no effort to explain that that would be the case! It seems to be the custom here in the South. Everything is breaded and deep-fried.

The Chinese restaurant in Fort Payne is one of my favorite local spots to eat. It offers a buffet with lots of choices of steamed vegetables, and steamed or roasted meats; and 1 can always find something that I like and feel is healthy cuisine. On the other hand, the buffet also offers a large selection of fried foods!

Now I really enjoy people watching, and I really enjoy watching what people take from buffet lines. (I guess part of that comes from the fact that I have been cooking for buffet lines for quite some time myself). Well, it is rather amazing (No it's not! I've got to find a different word, because it is rather self explanatory) when you watch the number of extremely obese people who line up and load up on nothing but fried cuisine. And then to see the amounts that some of them take!

I look at them and say to myself, "No wonder you're fat!"

I haven't found the courage to be rude enough to say it to their faces. Next to Mississippi-or is it Louisiana?—I forgot which, Alabama has the highest rate of obesity and coronary artery disease in the nation! Go Figure!

As we settled into our routine in Mentone and became acquainted with the owner of the aforementioned local restaurant, it amazed us one day when she was boasting about the quantity of used grease that the "grease recycling man" would pick up from her establishment each month. No kidding! She was proud of it! At the Hotel buffet, the only item that touched grease was our fried chicken, of which 1 am quite proud. But we didn't have enough used grease in a year to necessitate a single visit from the "grease man".

Another quaint custom, here in these parts, that you will find in restaurants, is on their menus. It seems customary here to offer various entrees with the choice of three or the choice of five "vegetables". Of course, five costs more than three. What I have found to be humorous is the choices that they offer for "vegetables". There are the obvious choices such as, corn, collard greens, beans, carrots, etc. And then, there are the not so obvious "vegetables" such as cottage cheese, applesauce, macaroni and cheese, ambrosia, peaches, pudding, and Jell-O.

HOTEL SNIPPETS

We had a couple show up one day who wanted to see our rooms. We were happy to comply. They explained to us that they were setting about the business of planning their vacation, and that they were going to visit all the spots on their itinerary and check out the facilities that they would use for their vacation. Now, what is the fun in that? Taking a vacation so one can plan one's vacation? I've never seen such a thing! I guess that they had no sense of adventure, or had extreme fear of the unknown-or both.

Then there was the lady who stayed with us who brought her own sheets! She stayed with us several times, and always brought her own sheets. They weren't silk. They were not 1,000-thread count. And to the best of our knowledge, she had no allergies. Go figure? To each their own.

Then there was the waitress who worked in the restaurant for us. She was confronted one day by an order for something she had never experienced-"Hot Tea". But to be undaunted, she proceeded to the kitchen and put some iced tea in the microwave!

Then there was the waitress who didn't know what an olive was, and referred to them as "those round black things". We had some guests with whom we were having a friendly conversation with around the fire one chilly evening. We were talking about recent restaurant humor and mentioned the "olive" incident.

Another guest who was nearby heard our remarks, piped up and said, "How dare you Yankees make fun of a Southern girl like that!"

I guess he had a "thorn in his butt" all along, and was just looking for something to complain about. Next thing we knew he checked out and disappeared into the night-all this before we had a chance to explain to him that we weren't Yankees, but "Western Cowboys", and that the waitress in question had just moved in with her relatives and had come from Minnesota.

And thank God for transom windows! On more than one occasion, when quests had locked themselves out of the room and had left the only key inside the room, we were able to boost a child through the transom window above the door so we could be let in.

And last but not least-and I'm sure I saw this a dozen times-were the people who asked to check the buffet before they paid. Of course they could. And invariably, each time, they had little Johnny in tow, who would make the decision for them whether or not to stay and eat. Many times it was "NOT"! Whatever happened to parental control? We always had a wide variety of tasty and nutritious foods to choose from, but I'll bet that they ended up down by the freeway at McDonald's.

WAITRESSES

We learned early on that a good waitress is hard to find. We also learned that waitresses in general were hard to keep. We also learned that a fair number of the girls who wanted to be waitresses seemed to think that we ought to be somehow beholding to them for just showing up. Good waitresses always seemed to have some reason or other to leave, and bad ones were for some reason let go. For starters, we had no place in our establishment for grumpy personnel. If they did not smile and treat guests nicely, they were out the door. I have found this to be universally true of most restaurants-waitresses seem to come and go as if there were a revolving door.

The "revolving door" comment I just made reminds me of someone who beat the odds. I had a dental patient in Fremont, California named Doris Baker who had worked for the same Denny's Restaurant for some 30 odd years. She is certainly an exception to the rule. But wait! The rest of the story! About 2 years after we moved into the Hotel, Bill and Doris Baker showed up in the lobby one Sunday afternoon. Turns out that they had just retired to Mentone and had heard about a "retired Dentist from California". They were too curious not to check it out. And sure enough it was their old Dentist-"Me"! What a small world!!

Now-a word or two about some of our favorite waitresses.

Brandy was young, thin, very cute, and very outgoing with the guests. She showed us early on that she was a "keeper". However, Claudia noticed that Brandy was wearing rather conservative clothes to work. (We didn't have uniforms, or a particular dress code.) Claudia took Brandy aside and asked her if she would like more tips. She did! The suggestion was made that she raise her hemline a little. She did and tips improved. She raised it a little more, and tips got even better. They even began to soar, especially with the male customers. Unfortunately, Brandy did not last more than a year. She was too cute and appealing to the young men, and one of them managed to spirit her away from us.

Holly is cute too. She has a very unique personality, and she is very talented in decorating things. We relied on her quite a bit to help us set up attractive arrangements of food and decorations—especially for wedding receptions and banquets!

Holly is also responsible for giving me my bacon recipe that has become my signature item as a B&B breakfast chef. Everyone, thanks to Holly, loves my bacon! I used to think that bacon had been misnamed-that it ought to be called "Fryon", because everybody fried it. But I learned better, thanks to Holly. It really is properly named-put a little brown sugar on it and put it on high heat in the oven and "Bake It"! Something wonderful happens when my bacon is bakin'! Although she didn't last long as a regular waitress, Holly was always ready to help out at special functions, wedding receptions, and banquets.

Shelia is Holly's Mother. She came to us by virtue of Holly and has become one of the special women we could call on to help at special occasions. She is a very nice lady and has maturity that comes in handy with the guests, as well as the experience. She has introduced us to her other daughter, Tammy, who also has helped us at group events.

Rosie! Now this is a special woman here. She came to us the first time riding on a motorcycle. She got off the bike, took her helmet off and all this hair fell out. Jacket off-and what a woman! Rosie is smart. She's been around and knows all sorts of old country ways. Rosie is all "woman" and every inch a lady-the one I really miss. "Rosie", Per Claudia.

Rub a Dub Dub... Two Waitresses in a Tub.

- Rosie and Holly -

(Rosie's Bike in Background)

Getting Ready for a Reception

WORKING HARD?

In addition to the limited restaurant business, our building proved to be one of the few in the area suitable for group events. In fact, group functions became one of our mainstays. Banquets and wedding receptions, we hosted quite often. In fact, one summer during the months of May to July, we hosted a wedding reception every weekend for 12 weeks in a row. All types-from sit down prime rib dinners to budget affairs featuring "pickles rolled in ham". (At the request of the young couple who were doing their reception on a shoestring. We did the whole thing for $100.00). May I draw your attention to an observation I personally made about these affairs? It seems to me that the more elaborate the reception, the more money that was spent-the more attention paid to impressing the quests, the less likely (in my biased opinion) was the marriage to succeed. It seemed to me that the less pompous the affair, the more genuinely in love the married couple appeared to be; and if I were a betting man, I'd put my money on them.

It was late on in the course of a reception. Guests were beginning to leave in fairly large numbers. Claudia and I finally had a chance to sit down and rest our feet at one of the tables near the entrance. We observed a young child hurriedly leaving the dining room. (Turns out he had been the ring bearer at the wedding-all dressed up in suit and tie-an adorable little boy I would estimate to be 4 or 5 years old max.) A few minutes went by and we observed him hurrying back into the room. As he entered the dining room, he slowed up at our table.

The gregarious little waif proceeded to rest his elbow on our table, prop his head upon it, look up at us and said, "Hi."

"Hi," I said back. "You seem to be a little out of breath." (He was panting.) "Have you been working hard?"

"No," he replied. "Pooping hard!"

What do I say back? I think I said something like, "That's nice," as he scampered off.

"Only out of the mouths of babes!"

How refreshing to see the lack of inhibition and the presence of forthright innocence that the young possess. This incident has caused me to reflect on society and the inhibitions that it often imposes, and it reminds me of the story of <u>The King's Clothes</u>, where it took a child to recognize that the King was naked.

In a separate incident that I remember well, a family entered the hotel lobby. The mother stated that "the children really had to go desperately bad and could I please point out the direction of the necessary facility". I reluctantly did so and began to walk away. As I did, I was surprised by the tell-tell clip clop sound of high heels. Peering around the corner, I saw the children sitting in the lobby as the mother disappeared down the hallway towards the "facility". To this day, I don't quite understand this one.

As long as were dealing with the "distasteful" topic, there are two other incidents that I find noteworthy on bathroom etiquette. Firstly, we hosted several women's groups for luncheons-such as the Garden Club, etc. Now these were not large groups, maybe 10 to 15 ladies. Our ladies' room had 3 stalls, and we would always keep them amply supplied with "T.P.". It seems no matter how hard we tried, that after every such event, there would be no "T.P." left! My wife could not understand it. Being a woman you would think that she could offer some input about the situation; but the best she could surmise was that they were either using a whole roll with each go, or else stuffing it in their purses for personal home use. We were finally made aware of the answer to the situation by one of our favorite waitresses. Rosie, being a southern girl, filled us in. According to Rosie, "fine southern women" use a technique that she described as follows-"WRAP WRAP WRAP WRAP WRAP WRAP WRAP WRAP WRAP WRAP WRAP WRAP WRAP WRAP-PAT"!

Lastly, there was the guest who asked for the use of a plunger before he went. I happen to know that there was nothing wrong with the toilet he used before he used it. This is one only for the imagination.

WE PICK OUR ROOM

We considered the whole Hotel our residence. We used the kitchen-the lobby as the living room-the shared baths. Yes! Shared baths! Back in 1884, having baths in the building was a luxury. No one thought of putting one in each room. There was one room on the first floor that we thought was cute. It was in the turret-light and airy-had a brass bed-but was rather small. We slept here for a few nights while we contemplated where we would stay permanently. We found it! On the second floor-the room right above the one we were staying in. It was in the turret-larger than the downstairs room-had more windows-was very light, and had an adjoining companion room. This would be our living quarters. We spent a whole day removing the junk. Luckily, this was the only upstairs room that had electric power. A local artist had used it a few years before as an art studio. Some paint, some carpet, a space heater, some curtains, and it became a very nice two-room retreat-except for the visitor!

It turns out that a section of ceiling had been stripped of its bead-board paneling. We had placed our bed under bare ceiling joists that sloped up to the attic.

The first night we slept in the room, Claudia elbowed me awake. "Dave, I hear a noise. It sounds like it's right over our heads."

I reached for my flashlight, shone it about at the ceiling, and to our surprise found a squirrel walking upside down on the joists above us on its way to the attic. Needless to say, my job the next day was to fill holes in the eves, and to board up the bare ceiling joists.

The attic was full of squirrels! We quickly acquired a young cat and placed her in the attic with food, water, litter box, and all the squirrels. In case you didn't know, squirrels don't like cats! They all disappeared in no time. Well, except the cat. We kept her. Turns out she was one of the best investments we made. We still have her. Her name is "Skitzie". As time went on, we regularly were reminded of the squirrels as we, in renovating upstairs rooms, would occasionally find a cache of nuts and acorns in a wall or floor space. I hope we didn't cause undue stress to the squirrels by depriving them of all this saved up food. A cat can, at times, be "man's best friend".

"Skitzie"... the squirrel cat

This Room Became our "sleeping quarters"

WE LEARN OUR LESSON-THE 3 R'S

Not long after taking over the hotel, Claudia took a phone call. It was a woman inquiring about the availability of the dining room for a PeeWee Football Awards dinner. Being anxious for some business, we decided to give it a go. A buffet was planned for "X" number of guests. The menu was altered to include such kid tempting dishes as, macaroni and cheese, chicken fingers, pizza, and Jell-O. You get the idea. We worked hard to get everything ready; and when the time came, things started out all right, but soon went down hill from there, and became what we refer to as the "Banquet From Hell"!

We had been told to prepare for "X" number of people, but when 40 more showed up than we had planned for, it created an awful mayhem in the kitchen! We were scrambling desperately to find, cook and put out more food. Meanwhile, those who showed up latest were being impatient and rude about the lack of food. It was the PeeWee people's fault. Not ours! But who do you think they wanted to blame? Meanwhile, out in the dining room, what started out as rowdy, turned into a virtual riot. Parents weren't watching their children. The kids were running about, yelling and screaming at each other, throwing and dropping food on the floor. And I'm not making this up. They were over in the corner having a "throw-up contest" by putting their fingers down their throats and gagging themselves. Where were the parents through all this? Just sitting by and ignoring what was going on. We were outnumbered! We did what we could, but without parent cooperation, it was a losing battle.

Claudia had identified the mother of one of the "thrower uppers", approached her and said, "Ma'am, your child is over in the corner making himself throw up."

Guess what the mother said? She said, "Well, I'm glad I don't have to clean it up."

As this was going on in the dining room, I was unaware. I had been running around the kitchen like a "chicken with its head cut off". I began to hear noises out in the Hotel lobby, and fortunately was done enough in the kitchen to leave and go see what was going on.

"Stop running!"

"Put that down!"

"Don't touch that!"

"Stop jumping on the furniture!"

"Don't go in there!"

"Where are your parents?"

At the risk of being accused of "child abuse", I even cuffed a couple of the non-compliant ones on the seat of the pants!

Where were the parents? They were all in the dining room visiting and not giving one bit of attention to their rowdy little brats. They had total disregard and disrespect for the Hotel premises and it's owners. We were glad to see them go, and we were unanimous in that! In hindsight, I wish I had been privy to all that had gone on in the dining room. Or perhaps it was best I didn't know, because I think I would have gone in there and done the best to throw the whole lot of them out! Never Again!! We were unanimous in that, too! We had learned our lesson. In all my experience with youth programs, and as a Scoutmaster, I have never seen the likes of this.

It is obvious that the parents here had no clue about the three R's. They had not taught them to their children, and it was totally apparent that they had not been taught them either. How can you teach what you yourself don't know? "Reason, Respect, and Responsibility." Without these three R's, I'm worried about the future of our great nation!

FLORA AND FAUNA

Talmadge Butler is the head ranger at DeSoto State Park, just 3 miles down the road from us. He commented one day that Lookout Mountain has more varieties of naturally occurring plants and animals than any place in the world! (Except for one place in China.) We have also found out, on good authority, that we have more varieties of trees right here than they have on the entire European Continent. We are blessed with nature! However, interestingly and pleasantly, we have very few mosquitoes. I think I saw one last summer-not too sure, but I think it was one. But we do have lots of other bugs and snakes and ferns and mosses and wild flowers and all that stuff. I have personally seen such animals as fox, wolf, coyote, beaver, deer, snakes of all sorts (including water moccasins), skunk, raccoon, bobcat, possum, box turtle, snapping turtle, ground hog, squirrel, chipmunk, and Canadian geese. I could go on, but I think you get the idea. I feel right at home here. After all, I am an animal, too. And I did major in zoology in college.

I previously mentioned the encounter that we had with the squirrels in the Hotel attic. One afternoon, we had an encounter with another visitor. Odie started barking his head off at something in the lobby. At first, we could not figure it out; but upon closer examination, we found a baby 'possum cowering behind a piece of furniture.

"What do we do?"

Having never encountered a 'possum before, it was not like, "Honey, will you please go get the 'possum bait and 'possum trap out of the cupboard."

Well, we thought a few moments, and hit upon the "cardboard box and a broom" scheme. It wasn't as easy as we would have thought, but with the help of several guests, in due time it was captured and released out in the woods.

Then there was the incident with the birds. I have no idea what prompted a small flock of them to fly down our chimney and out into the hotel lobby, but they did. This presented quite a challenge! We didn't have a bird net on hand in the cupboard with the 'possum trap, so we improvised again. Good thing the weather was nice-all doors and windows were propped open. After spending several hours shooing the birds around the lobby from ceiling fan-to ceiling fan-to ceiling fan-to ceiling fan, they all individually finally managed to find a door or window through which to escape. And we were quite pooped-not to mention the fact that we had also been pooped on!

Then there were the animals that quests brought. One of the most interesting guests we ever had was a woman who was apparently color-blind. Everything she wore was white-including her glasses, watch, and jewelry. Her luggage was white. Her hair was white. Her car was white. But in her car, in a large bowl, she did have two Goldfish. These were not white! The first thing she did upon arrival was request water for her fish bowl. Apparently, she had learned not to drive her car with the bowl full of water, or half of it ended up in the car. So she drove with it half-empty and re-filled it when she made a stop.

Finally, came the guests with two live Peacocks in the trunk of their Jaguar. Have you ever heard a Peacock screech? Well, if you have, you know what I'm talking about; and if you haven't, just be appraised of the fact that you have missed one of the loudest, most obnoxious noises on God's earth.

WHO ROOTS FOR WHOM?—OR MYOPIA

Alabamians are quite passionate about several things-Fishing, Hunting, and Auto Racing (Talladega), and COLLEGE FOOTBALL!!!! After all, the famous Bear Bryant coached here and Alabama was quite a football dynasty.

One afternoon at the restaurant, a 15 year-old employee (kitchen help), who was quite a good football player on the local High School team, asked the question, "Who do the football fans out West root for, Alabama or Auburn?"

(In case you don't know, Alabama and Auburn have quite a rivalry out here).

I thought about his question for a brief moment and then answered with a question of my own, "Who do the Alabamians root for, Cal or Stanford?"

(In case you don't know, Cal and Stanford have quite a rivalry out in California).

He looked at me. "Huh?" was his reply.

"You just answered your own question," I said.

"What?" he asked.

"Think about it," I replied.

Scratching his head, he went about his business.

I let him stew on it for a week and, when it was apparent he hadn't figured it out, I explained to him my answer. He was surprised to learn that there was a whole different world out there, and that Californians, in general, didn't give a "rat's ass" about Alabama football any more than Alabamians did about California football. I'm sure that his myopia will improve as he grows older and learns more about the outside world.

"ISMS"

The same young man mentioned in "Myopia" is probably responsible indirectly for this offering. We were talking one day about southern expressions, and the fact that every area of the country has its own peculiarities when it comes to manner of speech. We all can spot a good Boston accent. How about New York? Mid-Westerners are harder for me to spot. But in my estimation, Southerners really stick out! I mentioned to him that I thought the South was "more different" than the rest of the country. I really think I am right about this. Go to a book store or library and there you will find numerous books written on the subject of "Southernisms" but will be hard pressed to find anything on "Westernisms", or "Northernisms", or any other "Ism". (I do not intend to dwell on "Isms" for too long, because of the myriad of books out there that can be read; but I offer up a few of my favorites).

For example-"Y'all," I said.

"What's wrong or different about Y'all?" he asked.

"Well," I said, "It's not used anywhere else in the world-except in the South."

"Well, how do you talk to more than one person at a time without saying Y'all?" he asked.

"YOU," I said.

"You!?" he exclaimed. "You is only for one person.

"NO! I'm afraid to inform you, it's not! The word you can mean one person, or many people."

"No way!" he replied with astonishment.

I have no problem with Southerners using the word y'all. In fact, I use it quite often myself any more. I find it quite useful at times. What astonished me was that a seemingly, intelligent young man could reach the age of 15 and not have been instructed in the proper use of the word "You" by the southern school system!

"Unfortunately, the English language is full of inconsistencies and you just have to learn them," I explained to him.

One that comes to my mind is another kind of "you" spelled "ewe"", but is pronounced just the same. There is one Ewe-there are two Ewes. There is one Sheep, but then there are many Sheep. "SHEEPS" just doesn't sound right, does it? One of my favorite inconsistencies is as follows: I freeze, therefore, I am frozen-I sneeze, so obviously, I have snozen . Enough of this! Back to Isms.

One day, I was on the phone complaining about something, and the lady on the other end said, "Don't yell at me!"

"I'm not yelling," I said.

"Well, yes you are," she said.

"You must have sensitive hearing," I said, "because I'm speaking in a normal tone of voice. If you would like to hear me yell, I'd be happy to oblige you." The conversation went downhill from there. After the incident was over, it suddenly occurred to me that Southerners use the word "Yell" when they mean "Complain".

Another "Ism" I find interesting is "fixin'". We're fixin' to do this, or we're fixin' to do that. It means we are planning or intending to do something. The thought has occurred to me that if something needs fixing, all the "fixin'" in the world will do no good. I think "fixin'" is a good word for procrastinators.

Another one I like is "Carry". "We're gonna carry grandma to her doctor's appointment." ("Well, don't over-exert yourselves.") Simply put, "carry" means take. And the one that grinds on my nerves the most is "Suit"-I guess because I hear it constantly advertised on local TV stations and the radio.

"Come on down this weekend, folks-to our close out sale-and get yourselves a new living room or dining room 'Suit'."

I keep telling my wife that, one of these days, I'm going to take them up on it and ask if they have a size 52 men's jacket, with 38 waist pants, that I can purchase to wear in my living room or dining room? (By the way, that's my size jacket & slacks). I guess they never heard of a "suite" of furniture out here-pronounced "Sweet".

"Kwitcher yellin', little Buck, an' cumon. We be fixin' to carry ME Maw (grandma) to the store to get'a new living room suit."

After living in Alabama for eight years, I thought I'd heard them all! But No-o-o! Wal-Mart in Fort Payne sold me a riding mower that came up with a warranted defect. They sent me to a shop in Ider, a small town about a half-hour drive from here. I found the place and backed my pick-up up to the loading dock. The huge sliding door was open and I went inside to be greeted by, "Canfer?"

"What," I replied.

"Canfer?" he repeated.

"I'm sorry," 1 said.

"Canfer'ya?" he said.

"I'm sorry," I said. "I don't understand you."

"What can I do for you, Boy? You certainly ain't from around here ar'ya?"

"No," was my reply-asking myself if I should take offense at being called "Boy", since it was obvious I was twice his age. Feeling like a fish out of water, I decided not to take offense.

Well, a week later, I had a fully functional, totally repaired riding mower. I'm glad that they took care of my "canfer" by fixing my mower, and not just doing some fixin'!

WELL-IT LOOKS BETTER'N IT DID!

FINALLY! The signature chapter. The anticipation is over. I hope I can live up to your expectations; or I may lose you for the rest of my book, and any future babbling by me will be futile.

We were determined from the outset of this adventure that the Hotel would not become a money pit. Our pockets were quite shallow, so it could not have become one if it had wanted to. There were, however, some immediate problems that needed tending to-for starters the roof leaked. Hurricane Opal had seen to that. We fortunately found some shingles in the basement and set about replacing the missing ones. We didn't care if they didn't match! At least there were no more puddles on the dining room floor; and in our book, that was an improvement!

There was something else about the building that wasn't broke per se, but it was as ugly as hell; and we were determined to fix it. In our minds, it was screaming for attention-The Porch. It was a magnificent wraparound porch!—15 feet deep and 150 or more feet long. It had been rebuilt by the Padgets. The area under the porch was an "EYE SORE"! We thought about it for a few days. Then a light bulb lit up. I can't remember whose light bulb it was. I think I have to credit Claudia-Lattice!

We bought some 35 pieces of lattice-4x8'. I set up a painting table; and with a big fuzzy roller, was able to paint a piece in 5 minutes. White! They were then hung under the porch. Wow!! What a difference it made!

Our next-door neighbor, Jim Rotch, who owned the Hotel Annex-(Yes! I forgot to tell you that we didn't buy the "whole enchilada". In 1946, the annex was sold separately when Norville Hall moved in, and has a history of its own from that point on. It is now run as the White Elephant Antique Galleries).

"Well", Jim said, "You got more 'bang for your buck' with that lattice. It looks great."

Well, we thought so too; and our modest reply was, "Well, It Looks Better Than It Did."

"Well, It Looks Better Than It Did" became our favorite phrase as we made repairs and improvements.

"How does that look, Honey?"

"Well, It looks Better Than It Did," would be the reply.

When I finished painting the exterior white and green-(the existing colors were mauve and gray)-the original Hotel colors, we stood back and said, "Well, It Looks Better Than It Did."

We worked hard for 6 years putting heart and soul into the Old Lady; and I'm proud to say today, "Well, It Looks Better Than It Did."

This phrase has become one of our very favorites, and we have talked about having it engraved on my tombstone-with one little change-"Well, He Looks Better Than He Did!"

We knew that we could not make the Hotel perfect, so we didn't try. What we did do was a very good job. We created a great deal of improvement. Perfectionism has its place in this world-for example, space program, brain surgery, Olympic gymnastics (10)-but in everyday events, Life Is Too Short To Be Perfect.

WELL-IT LOOKS BETTER'N IT DID! 53

Lattice ... got a "Bang for our Buck"

MSH after we "fixed her up"

THE OLD OAK TREE

The parking lot was drab! It had no character. It did not present a good first impression to the guests, especially with a huge dead oak tree smack dab in the middle! It had to go! So, I set out one morning with axe and bow saw in hand to accomplish the task.

Our next door neighbor, who was looking on, asked. "Have you ever heard of a chain saw?"

I had. But I answered, "I think the exercise involved will do me good."

I started in on the tree and, about half an hour later, 1 felt like I was getting somewhere. I had worked my way over half the way through the trunk. Just about then, my son, Greg, came home from school for lunch. (Yes, my 15-year old son had recently decided to come and live with me and high school had just started).

"Dad," he said, "Please don't let it fall until I get home from school. I want to see it fall."

"Why not? After all, it isn't every day that one gets to see a big, old tree fall," I thought. So I put my chopping aside and set about doing other tasks. I would finish when Greg got home.

An hour or so after lunch, Jack Jones showed up-complete with some foreign dignitaries that he was showing the local sights to.

He asked, "Can they see the Hotel?"

I answered, "Of course they can."

I proceeded to take them on a tour of the building. About half an hour later, we went back out into the parking lot-and WOW! What a surprise! We had not heard a thing; but the tree was lying on the ground, having just missed the vehicles they had come in. (I can only surmise that we were on the far side of the building when it came down, since we didn't hear it). A stiff breeze had come up, and apparently was the "straw that broke the camel's back". When Greg came home, he saw the tree down and was immediately quite upset at me for having felled it without him. It took a little talking to convince him of what had really happened. I have tried to find something humorous in this incident, but I haven't been able to extract any humor from it.

Like I told Greg, "Shit Happens, and we should consider ourselves lucky that no harm came to the vehicles parked nearby."

I shudder at the thought of what could have happened if someone had been under the tree at the time. Luckily no one was injured.

Dead Oak Tree Site
Before (above) after (Below)

MENTONE

The first home built in the Mentone area was built by Robert Vernon in 1854. It is now the central portion of Saint Joseph's Episcopal Church.

In 1884, Alice Mason named Mentone. Her father was founder of the town. The French town of Menton is believed to be the inspiration for the name. Menton has been described as meaning "Musical Mountain Spring". Mentone was incorporated in 1936

The Little River flows through Mentone and is the only known river in this hemisphere to flow along the top of a mountain. Little River Canyon, near Mentone, is the deepest gorge east of the Mississippi River. There is evidence of Welsh constructed forts at DeSoto Falls dating back as far as 1482 AD. It is rumored that a Welsh explorer, Prince Madoc, sailed into Mobile Bay around 1170 AD. It is also believed that Creek and Cherokee Indians inhabited the area as far back as 8,000 BC.

Today, Mentone has some 500 odd inhabitants living within the town limits, and several thousand reside in the surrounding area. Today, the Mentone area has some 500 or so "odd" inhabitants, Claudia and I being two of the most odd! Well, we admit to being at least as odd as any of the others. Mentone is quaint, beautiful, scenic, tranquil, and weird. We have all types of weird people-us included-who live here. And some how, we all manage to peacefully coexist. We have "Old Timers", who's families have lived on the mountain for decades. We have artisans, authors, famous attorneys, doctors, lesbians, gays, Cherokee Indians, weird people from California, and a Buddhist Monk ordained by the Dalai Lama himself. And there is a rumor going around that we also have some practicing Druids, all living together in the Mentone area.

Something that we found out early on about Mentone is that almost everybody was either going to buy, or had a relative who was going to buy the Mentone Springs Hotel. It seems that people came to us, in droves, with one story or another about someone who had been on the verge of buying the Hotel at one time or another. I'm glad we bought it, because as far as I can tell, the other folks had just been "Fixin' to buy it".

Another thing that has occurred to me about Mentone is that, by far, the wide majority of folk who are in business in the town are from somewhere else-as is the case with us. There are a few businesses run by Mentone natives, but they are in a definite minority.

I would be remiss not to mention that the Mentone area is the "Camp Capitol of the South"-boys' camps, girls' camps, scout camps, church camps, equine camps-there are well over a dozen of them. It is estimated that 10,000 kids go to camp up here every summer.

I would also be remiss not to mention "Cloudmont Ski and Golf". Yes- a golf course with a ski slope-the southernmost ski area in the nation- owned and operated by Jack Jones and family. When the temperature drops, they make snow. There are usually about 90 days of skiing. And yes, I have been there on a clear winter's day, when you can see golfers and skiers doing their thing at the same time!

MOVING ON THE CHEAP!

I take a short pause from our story to put in a plug for Freight Brokers. This was something new to me. After deciding on the move, we contacted several moving companies for quotes. This was not going to be a "do it yourself move", as I have experienced many times in the past. A U-Haul wasn't going to work either. WE had too much stuff. The best quote we came up with was in excess of $8,000. We're Cheap!

I was discussing our dilemma with my brother and, bless his soul, he asked, "Do you know about Freight Brokers."

"No!"

Well they exist. And a walk through the Yellow Pages provided us with a contact.

Come moving day, they drop off one of those big cargo trailers in front of your house. You load it yourself. They haul it to your destination. You unload it. It cost us less than $2,000! What a savings! We had family and friends help us load it on the starting end, and we hired some help on the other end.

THE BIG FLICK

One day, a tall pretty young woman came into the hotel. She sought out Claudia and said, "We plan on making a movie here in Mentone, and we would like to use your Hotel."

"Sure," said Claudia, as she asked herself, "What planet did she come from?"

We had totally forgotten the incident, when about six months later, we were advised to attend the upcoming MAPA (Mentone Area Preservation Association) meeting. We did. The guest speaker was one Kyle Collins, husband of the young woman who previously had addressed Claudia about a "Movie". Kyle is an attorney from Birmingham. (He also had the distinction of being backup running back to Bo Jackson at Auburn University).

Lo and Behold! They did want to make a movie!! Turns out that Kyle's wife, Jamie, and a friend of hers, grew up close by. They had written a movie with the intention that it be filmed in Mentone. They had almost finalized a contract with a production company when the company reneged on the "To be filmed in Mentone" clause. So they went out and raised their own money and were going to, "On a shoe string", shoot the movie them selves, and would we please allow our facilities to be used free of charge?

"Well, what the hell! Why Not!" was the general consensus. Many locals acquired bit parts, including myself. (I appear for 3 seconds-no lines). Jack Jones got a speaking part.

Peter DeLouise, the son of Dom DeLouise, had the male lead. Jamie Collins had the female lead. The movie is <u>Southern Heart</u> and is a clean, southern, romance story. During the course of "the shoot", we allowed the actors to rehearse lines in the Hotel. We were also privy to helping put on a birthday party for Peter DeLouise. We were on a first name basis with

Peter, and as a "thank you" gesture, he had his father autograph and send us a copy of his cookbook, <u>Eat This-It Will Make You Feel Better</u>.

Many scenes in the movie were filmed in the M.S.H.; but not once do you know it, as the exterior of the building never shows up in the movie-so one really has no clue where the scenes were shot. (I guess 1 had done such a good paint job on the Old Lady that she looked too impressive to be allowed to be in the film, as I get the impression that they wanted Mentone to look a little more back-woods in the film than it really is). They were preparing to shoot a scene, and suddenly became aware of a "prop malfunction"-not really a malfunction as in "Janet Jackson". I'm just carrying on here. It was only a "prop omission". They had no telephone! What to do? Well, Dave "saved the day", by scurrying down to the Hotel basement and procuring an old black, bake-lite "dial" telephone that we had down there. It stars in the movie, and has a much longer time exposure on film than Dave got. I was hurt when they didn't mention my heroic effort in the credits.

It was an interesting and informative experience being able to see a movie made from such a close vantage point. Worth every penny of not being paid for the use of the building! But, 1 want my wind chimes back!! During the shooting of one of the scenes, it was quite late and quite windy outside. We had hung a very nice set of wind chimes (a gift from Claudia's daughter, Ginger) out on the porch. They had done a wonderful job of chiming, when the wind came up, for months on end. Seems they were "creating too much background noise". They got "disappeared" by a member of the film crew-never to be seen again.

About six months later, all of us who had contributed to the movie were invited to the Premiere Showing of the film at a theatre in Buckhead (Atlanta), Georgia. It was nice to see our names listed in the credits.

Peter De Louise with young movie participant

Dining Room Ready for Movie Scene

HONESTY HAS ITS OWN REWARDS

It was the third weekend in May. The annual Rhododendron Festival was in full swing. All the local businesses put on their best face. Craftsmen and other vendors set up booths at Brow Park. There is even a parade. Just to let you know, the Mentone area is famous for its wild rhododendrons. (We also have some domestic ones). Historically, they are at their peak of bloom during the third week in May. There are areas here that are absolutely gorgeous. One of my favorites is the bank of the river across from the parking lot at DeSoto Falls. Looking across, one enjoys a virtual sea of pink, mauve, and lavender.

We were highly caught up in the business of the Festival. Our dining room was stressed to the maximum with a huge lunch crowd. Buffet! Claudia was at the register and things were beginning to slow down a bit as a young girl approached her with outstretched hand and said, "Here, this must be yours. I found it on the porch." It was a roll of bills!

"No!" Claudia replied. "We aren't missing any money."

"Well, it must belong to somebody. You keep it and see if someone shows up to claim it," said the girl.

"Good idea," Claudia said. "However, I want your name and address in case no one claims it."

The girl's mother, who was standing close by, stepped forward and supplied the necessary information. They next proceeded to unroll the bills. There were 13 of them-all $100 dollars each.

Now!! How easy would it have been for the young lady just to slip the roll of bills into her pocket and take it home with her? It took real courage and honesty to do what she did. It would have been all too easy to evoke the rule of "Finder's Keepers".

We reported the finding of an undisclosed amount of money to the local authorities and asked them how long we had before we could claim it as our own. Three months! Well-we waited three months and no one claimed it. We phoned the young lady, and she was brought to the Hotel to claim it. Turns out she had been going to a private school, but her parents was hard pressed to finance this year, and she would have to go to public school. The $1,300.00 was just what she needed to make private school possible for her this year.

Nice Story, I think! Nice Outcome! We're glad we could have been a part of it.

SOUTHERN ANNOYANCES

I am taking on a touchy subject here, but I feel it important to express my observations and feelings. Having come from the West Coast, and been trained in Western thinking, I have found some cultural peculiarities that annoy me to no end.

"Where y'all from 'riginally?" is first and foremost on my list. It seems that Southerners are quick to pick up on speech patterns of those who are not "from here". If I have been asked this question once, I have been asked it 1,000 times! (And I don't think I exaggerate. Maybe I'm a bit conservative on the number). It seems that the phrase "where y'all from 'riginally", is probably the first sentence they teach young children here. It's somehow programmed into everyone's speech center in the brain. I've tried to be analytical about it, but I'm still not sure why southerners find this phrase necessary. I'm just guessing here, but it may be due to the fact that many Southerners don't seem to get around the country much. Born here-raised here-work here-and don't know much about any place except here. And, when they meet someone from somewhere else, they have to "break the ice" in some manner. I have been asked the question so-o-o-o-o many times that I really did once think of making up a sign and hanging it around my neck that reads-"Born in Utah, Raised in California".

On several occasions, I have replied, "Well, I was originally a gleam in my Pappy's eye." I thought I was being original and somewhat humorous, but quit that response when too many people looked down their noses at it.

Having been raised in another culture and having a different perspective, I feel it really doesn't matter one iota where someone is from. (Everyone on the West Coast is from somewhere else, so the question is totally mute). But what does matter is who a person is, what he does, and what he stands for. I'm biased of course, but I feel that the answers to these questions tell far more about a man than "Where y'all from 'riginally", and are topics for infinitely more stimulating conversation

Another question that gets asked almost as much as the "Where y'all from 'riginally?" question is, "How'd y'all get here?" This one bothers me too, but it's one I love to have fun with.

When someone asks me, "How'd y'all get here?" I usually answer, "Well, I got here twice-the first time by plane and the second time by car!"

This response usually creates a moment or two of silence, followed by, "No, that's not what I meant."

Then I say, "Well, that's what you asked. If you mean something else, feel free to ask it."

This is usually followed by another moment of silence, and some sort of clumsy explanation of what is really meant. What it boils down to is "What is your connection to here?" Or, "What made you decide to come here?" Or, "Who do you know here?" I find it really interesting the number of words and phrases that get used here in the South that mean something entirely different in the outside world.

"Southern Hospitality?"-Now that's another one that I am miffed about. I wish to relate another true happening. It had been a very busy Sunday buffet. We were dragging; and in spite of a mess of still dirty dishes to do in the kitchen, it was time to take a break. All of the guests had left, and there was no one in the B&B side of the business. (We seldom had guests on Sunday night). We put out the closed signs, locked the doors and settled down in the TV lounge. Boy, were we tired! We were tired of people! Just then, two "ladies" peeked their heads inside the back door.

"I thought 1 had bolted that door," 1 said to myself.

"I'm sorry, ladies. We're closed," 1 said.

"Well, we just wanted to see the old Hotel," one of them said.

I stood up and went to the back door to check and see if something had happened to the "Closed" sign. It was still in plain view where no one could not see it. By then they had barged on into the middle of the lobby.

"Didn't you see the closed sign?" I asked.

"Oh well, 1 guess not," the spokesperson said.

My initial urge was to escort them to the door, but thought, "Oh well, what harm can come from letting a couple of old ladies look at the place for a minute?"

Boy, was 1 wrong! They poked their noses into anything and everything. They asked questions about this and about that. Minutes became imaginary hours to me.

I really had just about had it, and had finally decided to tell them that "they were no longer wanted and it was time to leave," when the fatal question was asked, "Where y'all from 'originally?"

Well, that was the fatal question. I probably replied in a louder than normal voice, "Does it really matter where I'm from? I'm here and I'm having a good time."

"Well, how rude!" was the reply as they both marched themselves to the back door. I was glad that they finally found it under their own power.

"What ever happened to 'Southern Hospitality'?" they asked as 1 locked the door behind them.

I had learned in the course of my humoring them that they were from Birmingham. Well, a few days later 1 got an anonymous poison pen letter, postmarked from guess where?—Of all places, Birmingham! It doesn't take a rocket scientist to figure out who wrote it. The letter admonished me to go back where 1 came from "since there was no place for such a rude person in the south" and "1 needed a lesson in 'Southern Hospitality'."

Talk about "Southern Hospitality"? I call it "Southern Hypocrisy".

I ask, "Who was rude to whom?"

If the ladies had any common sense or decency about themselves, they would at least have said something like, "Oh, we're sorry. Please forgive our intrusion!" and then gone about their business. No-o-o-o-they ignored the sign, ignored my bringing attention to the sign, barged in anyway, and then made total nuisances of themselves. And they question my understanding of "Southern Hospitality"?

This incident does not stand alone! There have been others of similar proportion. The way I see it is, that "Southern Hospitality" means, "You wait on me, and I'll walk all over you, as I do what I want." I used to think that Southern Hospitality goes two ways, but evidently not. If what I have seen are true examples of "Southern Hospitality", then 1 want no part of it! I have found people everywhere I have gone, especially in Europe, to be equally or more hospitable than here in the south. Is "Southern Hospitality" a myth? Is it dead? Or, if it still exists, will I ever see it?

THE HONEYMOANERS

A young couple showed up one day looking for a room. They were on their "Honeymoon"-Very young, maybe just out of high school by my estimation. Well, we did have a room, but we also had a bunch of parents with kids who were going to check into camp the next day. Pretty much a full house. As previously mentioned, the old Hotel had very thin walls—single bead-board thick in many cases. As you can probably imagine, noise might carry quite well from one room to the next. Well it did! The next morning we were told by several parents that they had a hard time explaining what "all that moaning coming from the room down the hall" was all about.

Not wanting to embarrass the newly weds, who planned on staying another night, Claudia was quick to suggest that they take a long hike down at the park. They did, and things were a lot quieter that night.

SCOUNDRELS

When we moved to Mentone, we were told by some of the locals that Mentone was a very safe place to live. I have to generally agree with these allegations. We never lock our car, and nothing has come up missing. We leave valuable items in the back of the pick-up-wide open-in plain view that could be taken by anyone at any time; and we have never come up with something missing. I can't say the same for many places I have lived and visited. Things left out would have disappeared in the blink of an eye. It is a nice feeling knowing things are basically safe here. However, there have been a couple of individuals that we have met, that we would rather have not.

He booked a room at the M.S.H. and brought a lady friend to spend the night. A couple of weeks later, he booked another room with us and asked us on the phone, "When I come, please don't remember that I was there before?"

He spent the night with a different female partner. He did it a third time and, by now, we had become quite familiar with Less Hatch. He liked women. He liked alcohol, and made sure he always brought an ample supply with him, since we live in a "dry" county. He offered his libations to all-hosts and other guests alike. In fact, if one didn't know better, one might mistake the gregarious Less Hatch for the Hotel owner, the way he carried on with other guests.

The owner of the Mentone Inn, which is situated directly across the street from the M.S.H., was looking for a manager. One day Less called and booked a room. We were surprised when he showed up without a fourth different woman on his arm.

He explained that, "Tomorrow, I will assume the managerial duties at the Mentone Inn across the street."

Well he did! However, he forgot to pay us! Over the period of the next few weeks, I attempted to collect our money from Less. But he always had an excuse and "would pay me tomorrow". Well, this excuse making became very old, very quickly. One day, as I went out onto the porch, I spotted Less across the street in front of the Inn.

I yelled out in my loudest voice, "Less, when am I going to get my money?"

I did not care that he was in the presence of others who also heard my request. It worked! He paid me the next day! Good thing! Because Less skipped town about two weeks later. He had made off with a couple of months of receipts from the Inn. We heard through the rumor mill, that Less had "double dipped". Apparently, he had been telling guests that he was "holding their room with their credit card, but he wanted final payment in cash". He was not only using the card to "Hold" the room, but he was also charging the room to the card.

It was apparently when one of the guests became exasperated at trying to get the card charges reversed, that Less finally skipped town, with many thousands of dollars of the Inns' money. The "LAW" was after Less, but I never did find out if they caught up with him. I'm just glad we got from him what was due us before he left.

Claudia has suggested that I not use the name Less Hatch in this writing, because using "real names" could be touchy. But I reason, "Why Not!" Do you honestly think, for one minute, that "Less Hatch" was his real name? We often have heard the wisdom that "More isn't always better, and that sometimes Less is better than More". I haven't, in this instance, met Mr. More, but I can assure you that in this case, the odds are highly likely that "More is better than Less".

Our second scoundrel was a young man who had been doing a little work for the manager at the White Elephant next door. This was before Judy came along. We had bought a small house that was situated adjacent to the hotel, and had put it up for rent. The young man had approached us about the house. He "wanted to rent it for himself and his Mother".

We didn't feel good about this, and did our best to discourage him. Good thing we did! A few weeks later, the young man in our story and a male friend, whom we assume he had referred to as "his Mother", who happened to be wanted by the "law", were trying to hold up a couple just up the street from us. They had broken into the house and were threatening the older couple, when an accident occurred. "Mother's" gun went off accidentally, shooting the young man. "Mother" bolted from the scene. He was apprehended a week or two later. The couple was physically unharmed. The young man who "wanted to rent our house for himself and his 'Mother'" was dead!

OUT OF TOUCH-OR THE GENERATION GAP

The phone rang. It was a previous guest on the line. Did we have two rooms for Tuesday night? "Yes!"

In fact, we had no other guests that night.

"Good! Thank you. We'll see you then."

When they checked in, we recognized them immediately! Nice people! They had come up from Atlanta, which is only two hours away. The couple proceeded to introduce their daughter, (who's name fails me at this time) and her boyfriend Dave (who's name does not fail me at this time for obvious reasons you will see in a minute).

Our guests settled into their rooms. A while later they were off to dinner. I had started a fire in the lobby fireplace; and when our guests returned, they came in and sat around the fire. I struck up a conversation with Dave and, for starters, told him that he had a great name. Obviously because my name is Dave, too. We chatted quite a while. He had purchased an old mill, somewhere up in Virginia that he was renovating and turning into a residence. I told him about repairs we had made to the hotel.

After a while, I felt prompted to ask, "What do you do for a living?"

"Oh, I have a band," he said.

"Oh really! Do you get much business?" I asked.

"Yes. We're pretty busy," he replied.

The conversation went on for a while, having drifted onto other topics, and then it came back around, "What do you call your band?" I asked.

"The Dave Matthew's Band," he replied.

"Oh," I said, as a small light went off in my head. "I'll swear I heard that name somewhere before," I told myself.

The next morning, I asked my son Greg what he knew about the "Dave Matthews' Band". And the "shit hit the fan".

"How could you have been talking to the Great Dave Matthews down in the lobby and not come up and pulled me off my video game so I could come down and meet him?"

Oh Well!! I guess I had been out of touch.

HYPOCRISY

When Claudia and I got married, we told no one. We eloped to Lake Tahoe, found a wedding chapel, and it was "She, Me, and the Preacher". Some of our children took offense at this maneuver, and we were told so in no uncertain terms. They didn't like "being left out of the loop".

Well, seven years had gone by and we were still happily married. WE hadn't, either one, gotten the so-called "seven year itch". Many of our children were coming to visit us for Christmas.

So Claudia came up with an idea! "Why don't we renew our wedding vows in front of our children and grandchildren?"

"Why Not!"

So we set about making plans. There is a small chapel just down the road. We had on occasion attended church services in this building when lack of business allowed. We approached the reverend about our idea and he was positive about the proposition. . We made a small payment as rent to secure the use of the premises. Fortunately, I had the presence of foresight to ask the reverend for a copy of his wedding ceremony. He complied.

When I started looking at he "wedding ceremony", one thing was immediately apparent. It was To-o-o-o-o Lo-o-o-o-ng! Longer than we could have imagined! We had something "brief and to the point" in mind. Secondly, it was very preachy-full of scripture reading-this chapter and verse and that chapter and verse-and in some cases, what appeared to be almost whole chapters. And there was even some "Hell Fire and Damnation" thrown in. Of course, we didn't like it much, and knowing some of the guests who would be attending, we were absolutely certain that they wouldn't like it at all! So I called the reverend and told him my concerns. After all, we were just "renewing" our wedding vows.

"No!" was his reply. I will not shorten it!"

He would not alter it in any way! "Take it as is or leave it!"

"Okay," I said, not wanting to "burn any bridges".

We immediately started scrambling, looking for options. Bless his soul, an acquaintance of ours who is an ordained minister agreed to do it the way we wanted it done.

The next day, I called the reverend on the phone and thanked him for his willingness to do our ceremony for us, but told him he was "Off the Hook", as we had found someone else to do our ceremony.

The next day the blessed reverend called us back. Claudia answered the phone, and he said, "Now, I don't want any 'Heathens' in my church! We're 'Christian' you know, and we don't take kindly to Heathens using our church!"

Well, I almost called him back to ask him, "Whom do you think Christ preached to? The Christians? There weren't any 'Christians' at the time of Christ! Only Heathens who accepted his teachings and later became known as Christians."

Well, I let it pass. Do I sense a small bit of hypocrisy here? No, it couldn't be, could it? Not in a "Christian church!" I'm sure the good reverend doesn't allow hypocrisy in his church any more than he allows "Heathens".

Well, to make a long story short, we had a nice, simple ceremony, and renewed our vows in front of our children, in spite of those "Heathens" that were present! And I'll bet you can guess what church we haven't been back to since!

HOW CAN DRYNESS BE SO WET?

We live in a "DRY" county! We've lived here for 9 years now, and we're still not sure what the term "Dry"" means. For one thing, alcohol can't be sold here. But that doesn't appear to mean much, because "Boy oh Boy" does it ever flow here! I've lived in many different places, but never in my life have I seen so much alcohol consumption. It seems that most everyone here drinks. I'm one of the few exceptions! I can't stand the stuff. I could drink alcohol if I wanted to, but I find the rotten stuff offensive to my taste.

I'm a non-drinker, who lives in a "Dry" county, but Boy Do I Wish It Were "Wet"!

We have an "Adopt a Mile". You know we clean up litter for free because it looks ugly, is offensive to our environment and to us, and nobody else will. It seems that many of the locals think it is their "God given right to pollute". There are however a few environmentally conscientious individuals who live here and they have "Adopt a Miles" too, bless their hearts. I do not exaggerate when I tell you that well over half of the litter we collect is alcohol-related. Mostly beer cans and bottles. Never have I seen such alcohol-related debris anywhere I have lived! Why do you suppose that is?

Well, we live 5 or 6 miles from the Georgia border, where it isn't "Dry". Strategically placed, just feet across the state line, stand two stores that specialize in guess what?—Liquor! What a coincidence!

Now why would that be? Do you suppose that people from our county drive over there and buy it? And do you suppose that those same people drink it in their pick-up on the way back, so as not to get caught? And do you suppose that they throw the bottles out the window also, so as not to get caught? And who gets to pick them up? You guessed it, me and Claudia and all those other good folk who live here and give a damn!

And who do you suppose now has a blood alcohol level that is too high, while driving home? I have not researched the specific numbers, but it seems to me that we have more than our share of DUI related accidents and deaths in this county.

The local churches here seem to have enough political control to have brought about legislation banning alcohol, but all the preaching they do seems to fall on individual deaf ears. What I find saddening in all this is the fact that this county is not financially well off, and it is losing all that revenue, and taxes as well, to Georgia. Our schools are under-funded, and so are a lot of other programs. Contrary to what the local churches teach, I have lived in wet counties all my previous life, and I feel less safe here. People in "Wet" counties seem to me to have a lot more common sense about alcohol use than they do in "Dry" counties where drinkers have to "Hide" their habits. It's safer for everyone when you don't drive home drunk.

One of the most interesting events that we ever hosted at the M.S.H. was a semi-annual buffet dinner banquet for a group of retired DeKalb County citizens. (Since it was semi-annual, and since they liked us, this event was held a number of times in our dining room.) The group would schedule dinner for a certain time, but they would always show up an hour early. They would be toting boxes and bags and coolers, and since we have a "Dry" county here, we didn't know anything about what was brought. They set something up in the corner of the dining room, with such things as whiskey, rum, scotch, bourbon, wine, vodka, and the like-no beer! Beneath their dignity I guess. By the end of the hour, they were all very "happy". Actually many of them were on the verge of being stone, cold drunk.

The dinner always went exceptionally well! No problems! We always had nothing but compliments from those who dined on our buffet offerings. I told Claudia it was because they were too drunk to care.

There is something I was dying to do, but Claudia restrained me. I wanted to go out during the meal and make the following announcement, "Ladies and Gentlemen, if I could have your attention for just a moment please! I would like you all to show me by the raising of hands, which ones of you voted in the last election to have this county stay dry?"

I'll bet you dollars to doughnuts, that if they were honest folk, as I expect them to be that, to a man, they would have all raised their hands!

RACE

I'm not talking about something here that may involve a contest to see who can drive a vehicle or run the fastest. I'm taking on a touchy subject here, but I feel I must, because it belongs to our story. I grew up on the West Coast. I have had many friends, schoolmates, bosses, and co-workers, who were not Caucasian, for whom I have nothing but total respect. It is however a total shame that some people don't care to judge others based on their individual merits, but tend to categorize, characterize, minimize, patronize, criticize, ostracize, dehumanize, and despise them based solely on skin color, social, cultural, or even religious differences. Aren't we all members of the human race? Aren't we all God's children?

We quite often get asked, "Wow! Wasn't that a cultural shock for you to move from the West Coast out to Alabama?"

And we usually say, "No! Not really. It's not really as great a difference as you think."

But this one issue has been for me the biggest shock! I would have thought, that after having much of the Civil Rights Movement centered right here in Alabama (Rosa Parks, Martin Luther King Jr., the march on Selma, etc.) that Alabama would have changed the most. Here in Northeast Alabama, however, they have seemed to change the least.

My wife tells me I ought to "leave this one alone", but I'm too stubborn. It's real and it happened! Claudia doesn't want us to be the recipients of a "cross burning" on our lawn. (The K.K.K. is still active in these parts.) If we get one, I'll let you know! Now here are some true stories that I still have a hard time believing.

Shortly after our arrival in Alabama, an acquaintance of ours was showing us around.

"Do you see those trees over there," he asked as he pointed to a grove of Southern pine.

"Yes we do," we replied.

"Well, do you know what we call them?" he asked.

"No," we responded.

"We call them 'Nigger Pines'," he said. "Do you know why?"

"No."

"Cause they ain't good for nuthin'."

I was shocked at how openly and blatantly racist he was.

He then boasted of the fact that, "No 'Niggers' live up here on the mountain. Do you know why?"

"Why?"

"Because they are afraid of what would happen if they did!"

One Sunday, at our buffet, a woman asked if she, in addition to her meal, could have a to-go box. We generally didn't give out to-go boxes, but she was nice, and, "What the harm would it be anyway?" So we fetched her one.

"Well, thank you very much," she said as she began filling the box. "It's for my maid who is waiting outside in the car."

"Well, why don't you bring her in here?" Claudia asked.

"OH, NO! You don't understand!" she said, as she continued to fill the to-go box. "You wouldn't want her in here. She's black."

Then there was the only occasion that we were ever asked by a local concern, "Will you put up a Travel Writer from the West Coast who is working for Mercedes Benz?"

"Of course we will!" was the response.

After he showed up as our guest for the night, I began to put two and two together. I asked Claudia if she had a clue why we were asked to put up this nice fellow, when there were any number of facilities who were much closer to his center of concern? She had seen it too. "Of course," she said. "Because he's black! No one else in the area would take him, and they knew we would."

There are more incidents and comments that I could write about on behalf of this topic. Here's a short one.

I heard this comment one day. "I don't have anything against 'Niggers'. I think everyone ought to own one."

Enough said! I'm going to let it rest now. You can be the judge whether or not racism still is going strong in the south.

You'd a thought that along with "dryness", the religious zeal and fervor here could have legislated racial equality.

"GOOD OL' BOY SYNDROME"

We had done business in Mentone for approximately 5 years. We had done our banking down in Fort Payne at AmSouth Bank. So when the occasion presented itself for us to "need" (want) a small construction loan, the purpose for which, I will tell you later, we went to our bank thinking that a small loan would be a "slam dunk" proposition! After all, we had run hundreds of thousands of our business dollars through the bank's coffers. We would put up the Hotel as collateral.

Much to our surprise and dismay, we were turned down for no obvious reason! I should say Claudia was turned down, because she owns the Hotel and was applying for the loan. We couldn't believe it!!! The Hotel was worth a lot more than the $20,000 we were asking for. The county tax commissioner, whom we personally know, told us that she thought the land alone upon which the Hotel sits would sell for in excess of $100,000.

But what we found really odd during the loan application interview, was that the loan officer kept looking and talking to me when it was Claudia who was applying for the loan. After the loan rejection took place, Claudia's West Coast financial adviser got wind of the rejection and out of no urging by us, he took his own initiative and called the bank officer and told him that he was crazy not to have made the loan. It made us feel a little better, but it didn't solve our problem.

Well, we don't give up easy!!! So, to be undaunted, we "hiked up our bootstraps" and went on. Each bank that we went to gave us the same treatment. The officer always spoke and looked at me, ignoring the fact that it was Claudia who was applying for the loan, and in the end we were turned down.

"Well…It Looks…Bettr'n It Did"

I remember well the comment by the pompous idiot down at the bank in Valley Head, who said, "Well, some people think old hotels are worth something, and then some do not."

Well, we do not give up easy!!! So to be undaunted, we went over the border into Summerville, Georgia. We went to Farmers and Merchants Bank where the "red carpet was rolled out" for us! We had never banked there, but they gave us the kind of treatment that we expected we would have received at AmSouth. Now, why do you suppose Claudia was treated so poorly in Alabama? It has a lot to do with the customs and the "Good OL' Boy" syndrome. Since she was a girl, she didn't qualify. Like "Nigger Pines" it appears that women in business "Ain't good for nuthin'". Oh yes, women have their place in DeKalb county, but being in business isn't one of them. We have, since this incident occurred, spoken to several women in our area, who run businesses here, and they all have had similar experiences, and they bank in Georgia. Where do we bank? In Georgia, of course! It has been suggested that we report the discrimination that Claudia received, based on her gender; but it wasn't worth the trouble to us. They'll get theirs in due time. Things have a way of "coming around" after they "go around".

THE ROOF

After living in the hotel for about two years and patching the roof as patch can, we decided it was time for a new roof-the biggest expense we would incur while running the Hotel. So we let our "Fingers do the walking through the yellow pages", and we started calling roofers. There were about a dozen or so listings. We got everything from a mixed response to no response at all. Out of all the listings called, we did eventually get one roofer to come out. He didn't want the job "Because the turrets were too steep". We had received promises that roofers would come out, but none other materialized. Approximately six months had elapsed, and nothing!

What an eye opener! We could not believe the lack of interest, or ambition that was shown towards our roofing job. The money was green!! But we have found through experience that that is more or less the norm around these parts. Not unlike the waitress situation, it appears that many workers here in these parts feel you ought to be beholding to them for just showing up. And after they get paid, don't look for them until the money you paid them has been exhausted on beer and cigarettes. The sense of competition we had experienced on the West Coast just didn't seem to be present here. Were I on the West Coast needing a roof, it would have taken only a couple of phone calls and the problem would have been solved. But unfortunately I was not on the West Coast.

So we started expanding our search! We were beginning to get a little anxious about not finding someone, and were on the verge of calling roofers in Georgia and Tennessee, when out of the blue, we had someone show up on our door step. "I see that you need a roof," he said. "I'm a roofer, and would like to give you a bid."

Of course we asked him what ever gave him that idea? And told him that he was dreaming if he thought we needed a roof-"NOT"! We almost fell over backwards with astonishment.

"Bless you, Bony Phillips!" That is his name, and roofing was his game, and yes we struck up a deal!

Now, before I go on, guess where Bony came from? Georgia of course!—Summerville, Georgia, where we do our banking now. (If we didn't love it so much here where we live, I think Georgia might be a good alternative choice. It seems to be a state where people get things done.) Someone had found us!! And to think I had almost lost my faith in miracles.

Bony Phillips and his crew did a very nice job. They were good and efficient, and cleaned up their mess. What "blew me away", was the way his crew worked on the turrets without the aid of safety lines. They just nailed 2x4's up and walked on them. As you can see in the accompanying pictures, the turrets are very steep.

About half the way through the job, Bony took us aside and said to us, "You know, this roof wouldn't have had to been re-done had the previous "Roofers" done it right. The shingles up there are perfectly good, had they only been nailed with roofing nails and not shot with a staple gun, and had the roofers nailed on the nail line where they are supposed to, and not just top nailed the shingles. In other words, the Padgets, who paid for the previous roof, had been "took". Some of the locals we talked to had recalled to us the drunken parties that took place amongst the previous roofers; i.e., they had been drunk while working on the roof.

Needless to say, Our opinions of the local work ethic were not bolstered by the roof experience. And we have not had much happen to change our opinion. We have found out that there are a few good men up here who take pride in their work and do a good job. They are few and far between, and hard to find, but they do exist. We had a very pleasant experience with a local builder named Steve Davis, some time later on; and I will recommend him to anyone who wants a good job done in an efficient manner. Also, I stand in awe of David and Cheryl Baker who run "The Shed Nursery" near Mentone. They are very hard workers. But basically it has boiled down to the fact that if we want a good job done in an efficient manner, we do it ourselves, even if we have to educate ourselves in the "how to", and buy the necessary tools to do it.

THE ROOF 87

Borys' crew on the turret

GREAT EXPECTATIONS

Valley Head High School is where my son Greg went his last 2 years. Valley Head is a small town just down the mountain 3 miles from Mentone. When it came time for graduation, we were excited for Greg and for his friends who would graduate with him. Greg was in a graduating class of some 25 or so students.

When we showed up at the football stadium for the ceremony, we couldn't help but marvel at how packed it was. How could 25 students attract so many well-wishers? Of course we had based our observation on what we knew from our own graduation experiences.

The "pomp and circumstance" far exceeded anything we had seen at a high school graduation. The individual candidates were introduced one by one, and quite a thorough sketch was given about each student. Of course when you take into consideration that there were only 25 grads (where we had gone to large high schools with hundreds of grads), it made sense that more time could be allowed for each individual.

When they started getting into "future plans" of the individual students, that is when the light lit up. When I graduated from high school, over half of my class was going on to college. Valley Head Class of 1997, as it turns out, was sending only 3 of its grads to college! That's not one-half, or one-fourth, or even one-eighth-it's less than that. This graduation was for the majority-the culminating event in the academic careers of those involved. And therefore, rightly so, deserved the pomp and circumstance. There were no other expectations!

Another shocker, for us at least, was what happened at the Homecoming Football Game. It was time to introduce the Queen! Well, of course Miss First and Second Runner-Ups were introduced first, with the usual expectations-"This is Miss So and So. She has a 4.0 GPA. Her favorite class is underwater basket weaving. Her favorite color is green. She plans to-whatever. Her favorite activity is whale watching. She is escorted by her father."

Now came the Homecoming Queen-"Introducing Mrs. Jones."

Yes! MRS. Jones. (I leave out the real name.) "Her favorite activity is playing with her 1 year old son. She is escorted by her husband."

We were stunned! We had always thought of a Homecoming Queen as a "Miss". Well, what can you say? Her classmates voted her to be Queen. And you have to hand it to the girl for having continued on in school until graduation!

ALL GOOD THINGS MUST END

Well, there almost always seems to be good news and bad news. Our good news is that we got so busy at the Hotel, that we couldn't handle it. The bad news was that we couldn't find help that we considered good and reliable, and we were running ourselves into the ground. This was partly due to the nature of the business.

There were times we were so busy that we wished people would go away; and then, there were times when we wondered if we'd ever see any more business, which we inevitably did; and it got so busy we wished people would go away. The dilemma was that we couldn't keep it up without making a change. Do we keep on looking for help? Should we quit altogether? Should we do something else?

After giving the situation some due analysis, we decided that the part of the business we liked the most was the B&B. We were unanimous in that! It would have been a shame to limit the M.S.H. just to B&B business. It was too good a facility for banquets, receptions, and the like. So, as much as we loved the Old Lady, we decided it was in our best interest to let her go and pursue a B&B only career.

Knowing full well that a buyer for our business might not be right around the comer, we put her on the market and waited patiently. (We hoped the buyer was right around the corner, but he wasn't). So we patiently waited. It isn't every day that someone wants to buy a 100+ year old hotel. We had quite a few lookers, but no immediate takers.

We have, it seems, an optimistic streak in our bones. So we initiated a search for a piece of land upon which we could build a brand new B&B. We have seen a few B&Bs in our day, and all of them had been converted from an existing building. Usually, the conversion process worked, but left something lacking. We had decided to pass on the "conversion" idea and build a B&B from scratch. After searching for a few months, we found it!!—A beautiful 45-acre parcel-5 acres of water-20 in grass-20 in woods. The mobile home, old rickety-barn and other old structures could go.

We were right! We got rid of all the old stuff, built a new 5,500 square foot B&B; and we're darn proud of it. We have a huge (1,600-sq. ft.) great room with fireplace, library area, TV area, and pool table. We have a hot tub outside. The rooms are all spacious and unique, and there are only 4 of them! The baths we did ourselves from scratch. One of them has a waterfall shower. One has a rain cloud that rains on you. The "Garden Room" has a watering can for a shower.

The eventual sale of the Hotel made us enough profit to do what we wanted to do. We now have a much easier schedule and are really enjoying entertaining the guests. We also enjoy the associated yard work, do gardening, and have chickens and rabbits. Business is very good and we're pleased as punch. Our place is known as Crystal Lake Lodge. Next time you're in Mentone, stop by and pay us a visit.

The sale of the M.S.H. was slow, and the escrow period proved to be a very unsettling experience. Some of the things we agreed to, we found out through sad experience, we shouldn't have agreed to. It taught us a lesson in what not to do.

At the close of escrow, the new owner made some unkind remarks along the line that we had better get out immediately, or else. My reply, "Well, in case you didn't know, Alabama law gives the seller thirty days to vacate the premises!" It shut him up! We didn't want to be there any more than they wanted us to be there. We were gone in two days!

Isn't it nice to be able to learn from experience? But she was sold, and that's what's important. The new owners continue to improve on the building where we left off and that makes us feel happy.

Forest Room: Crystal Lake Lodge

Garden Room

Scene from Crystal Lake Lodge in the Fall

"LET ME MOW ON IT"

As I have previously mentioned, we now own 20 acres of grass. Fortunately, about 10 of it is in pasture and we let the Llamas and the Horses mow it for us-the other 10 or so gets mowed by us. We have "His" & "Her" riding mowers. Now, you may find this hard to believe; but we fight over who gets to mow. Nothing violent, of course! But we both like mowing so well that when business requires one of us to stay near the phone, or take care of other domestic duties, when we both can't mow simultaneously, things get a bit competitive.

In case you didn't know, Alabama is terminally green. We get over 60 inches of rain each year, and if we go for over two weeks without it, the locals start talking about a "drought". One day at the Hotel, some ladies were talking about their "poor flowers starting to wilt, for need of rain".

I had occasion to ask them, "Have you ever heard of a water tap and hose?"

Seems folk around here don't give much thought to watering their plants. Where I grew up, everything needed watering or it died. Here in the South, I was surprised to see how trees seeded themselves, and if one didn't mow down the seedlings one's lawn would soon be one's forest. In the warm part of the year, it is basically like a big "Green House", and sometime the grass grows so fast that one mowing a week isn't quite enough.

Well, in case you didn't know, mowing can get quite monotonous-back and forth, up and down, side to side, round and round, crisscross, figure "8's"-there's only so much one can do to try to break the monotony. Your butt also gets sore after a few hours. Also, if you don't wear earplugs, the engine noise will create a good "Ringing" in the ears!

So-Why, do you ask, do we fight over it? Because it is also very therapeutic! Yes! Very Therapeutic! Am I nuts or what, making such a claim?

No, I don't think so. I offer this observation only out of first-hand experience. Ask Claudia. She'll tell you the same. That's why we "fight" over mowing. The mower, after a while, learns it's routine and one doesn't need to steer it. It sort of takes care of itself. The mowing business therefore gives me lots of time to think! To Reflect! To Analyze! It's sort of like meditation—mentally and spiritually refreshing. I have come up with many of the thoughts that went into this book while mowing. If I had not had the chance to mow, I doubt whether or not this book would exist.

When there is something about which an important decision must be made, I always now tell my dear wife Claudia, "I'll give you my thoughts and decision about it later. First Let Me Mow On It!" In fact, "Let M Mow On It" just might be a good title for my next book. I had considered it for this one.

Now, you may wonder what happens in the winter when the grass don't grow and we don't mow. Well, that's when we set aside all-important decision making; and we go into the "Fixin'" mode. We do our best to be "fixin'" to make our decision till spring rolls around. Then we "MOW ON IT"!

Thank you for reading this little story of mine. Had we not made the move to Alabama, I think our lives would have been infinitely more boring. I'm glad I could share these experiences and thoughts with you. I guess I'm done now with my composing. I hope I can find someone to publish it, so you can read it before I start decomposing.

978-0-595-35477-1
0-595-35477-7

LaVergne, TN USA
22 May 2010
183437LV00004BA/3/A